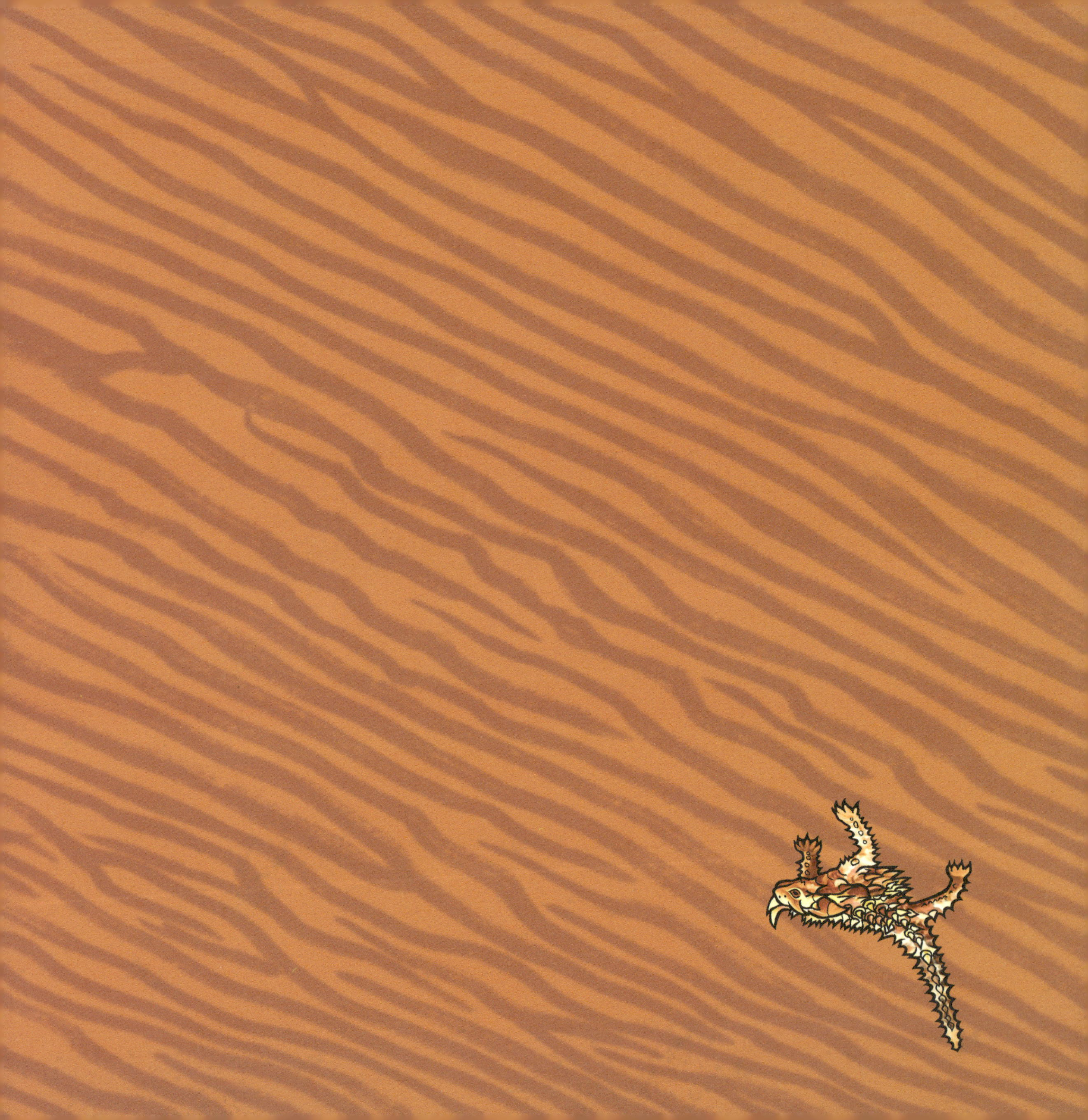

OZ
ANIMALS

Z ANIMALS

Written and illustrated by

Andrew Davies

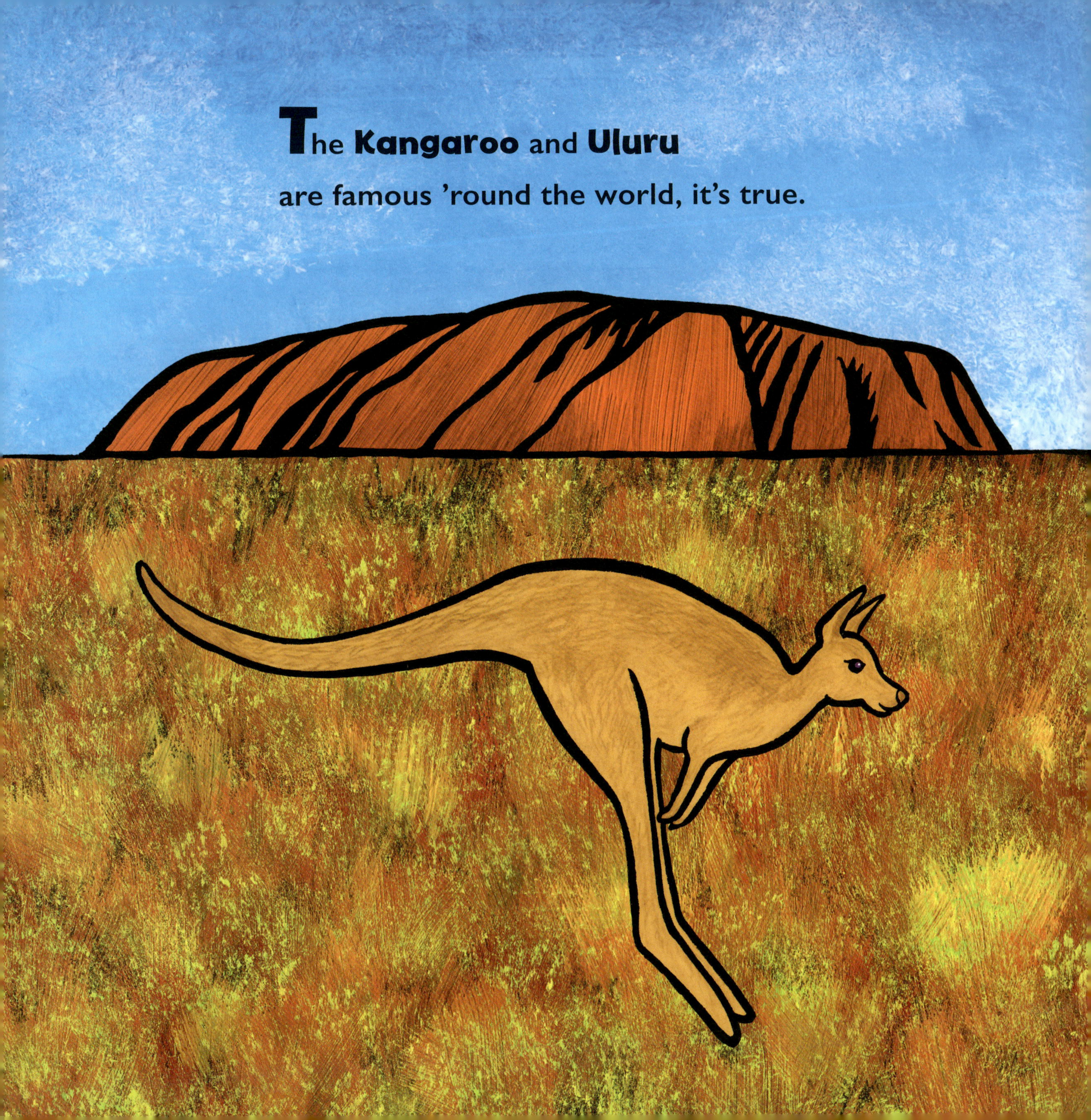

The **Kangaroo** and **Uluru**

are famous 'round the world, it's true.

But do you know the **Potaroo**?

The **Wallaby**
or **Wallaroo**?

The Land of Oz where you can view:

a **tongue** that's long,

a **tongue** that's blue,

a **Sulphur-crested Cockatoo**,

an **Emu** or
a **Jabiru**.

There's such a lot that you can do.
There's something here for all of you.

A lovely **Rainbow Lorikeet**
will chat with me at times we meet.

And when there is no more to say
she spreads her wings and flies away.

The furry duck-billed **Platypus**
is nothing like an **Octopus**.

It's nothing like ...
well, here's the thing:
it's really not like **anything!**

A Numbat will be happy
when he finds a **Termite mound**
for **Termite mounds** are places
many **Termites** can be found.

A **Numbat** eats quite happily
a thousand **Termites** raw;
then after, just as happily,
will eat a thousand more.

The **Numbat** may then rest while he
avoids the mid-day heat,
but after that he will be back
for thousands more to eat.

From the bush we heard a sound,
and so we stopped and looked around.
"I think I heard a **Lyrebird**."
"A **Lyrebird**? Now that's absurd!"

The sounds we heard went: **Cheeep Cheeep Choo** 
and **Wee-wah Wee-wah! Wooo-woo-woo!**

Kook-
Kook-
Kook-
Kook-
Kook-a Koo

Buzzzz Buzzzz Buzzzz Buzzzz Buzz Bazoo

And then
out popped the **Lyrebird**
repeating to us,
word for word:

There's a rustle and a bustle
coming high from up the tree,
And it's possibly a Possum
or a family of three.

I hear no funny screeches
so I know it's not a bat.
It's not like utter silence
so I know it's not my cat.

It's probably some possums,
though it's somewhat hard to see
when they're hiding in the blossoms
in the dark and up a tree.

Down in a hole there was hidden a ...
... something odd – and I'm not kiddin' ya –
an egg-laying mammal enigma:
the spiny ant-eating **echidna**.

Be wary of the **Cassowary**.
Head like rock and feathers hairy.
Has a kick that's rather scary.
So we say be very wary.

Any **Goanna** that's trying to flee,
finds **something** to climb
that is tall –
like a **tree**.
And never considering
what that might be,
just has to find something
– that *something* was **me**!

When **Crocodile** hatchlings together start hatching,
the **Crocodile mother**, not biting or scratching,
will pick up her babies, all safe in her jaws,
then off to the river she goes on all fours.

Say, have you ever considered
the wonderful **Frilled-neck Lizard**?
He opens his frill and gives such a great thrill
that you might think this lizard's a wizard.

The original Australian rebel
is the terrible **Tasmanian Devil**.
He's small but he's tough,
and he's mean and he's rough
and with whom you just **don't** want to meddle.

Wombat smiled at Bowler **Bilby**
"Look out, lad, for soon I will be
showing off my many tricks.
Now watch me hit that ball for **six**!"

But **Wombat** had to take his bat
and cricket pads and baggy hat,
and wander back to where he sat
when **Bowler Bilby** called:

"Howzat?!"

Once a lonely **Kookaburra**
left her nest in Turramurra,
looking for her long-lost **mother**,
last seen out in Tibooburra.

On the way she met her **brother**
(one without the duller colour).
Brother also missed his mother.
Up he flew from Ulladulla.

Meanwhile, back in Tibooburra,
father sadly said to **mother**,
"How I miss my Kookaburra
little baby and her brother."

And the **Mother Kookaburra**
always hoped they'd see each other;
prayed that one day or another
they'd come back to Tibooburra.

Then, you know what happened after?
Flying in with joy and laughter.
Father, **mother**, **sister**, **brother**,
home again with one another.

Koalas in a gum tree.
Joey counting **sheep**.

Koala eating **gum leaves.**

Joey falls asleep.

For Ken and Jan

and the Australian spirit

Also in this series:

Published in 2025 by New Holland Publishers

newhollandpublishers.com

ISBN 9781760798086

Managing Director: Fiona Schultz
General Manager/Publisher: Olga Dementiev
Designer: Andrew Davies
Production Director: Arlene Gippert

Keep up with New Holland Publishers:
NewHollandPublishers
@newhollandpublishers

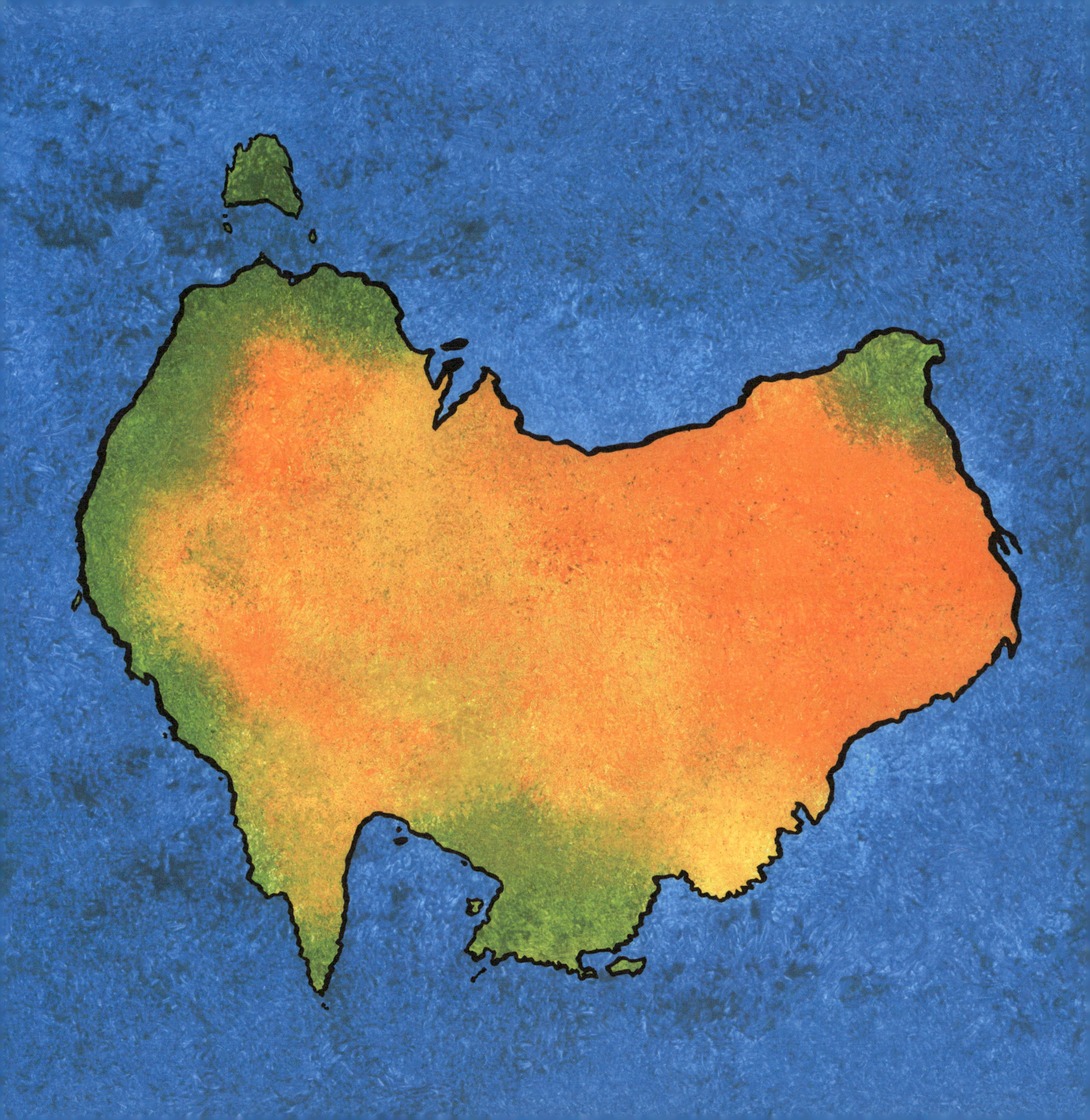